The Dove's Lesson

By Margaret Henderson

DEDICATION

To Mothers

The Dove's Lesson

In a mess of a nest
In the fork of a tree
A white wing-tipped dove
Taught her lesson to me.

The Dove's Lesson

Intent she did sit
Til her feathers they ruffled.
Amazedly I watched
As the Mother uncovered...

The Dove's Lesson

Two scrawny heads,
Wiry necks, folded wings.
Before me they peaked
From their home of bark strings.

The Dove's Lesson

Two baby doves nested
Safe and secure beneath Mother's wing.
Their future uncertain
Without her care most extreme.

The Dove's Lesson

Food was flown in as if catered
And served by the dutiful Mother.
How patient she was throughout
While she gave constant cover.

The Dove's Lesson

Soon the Mother's wings spread often
For the breeze and the sun
To greet and entice
Her little loved ones.

The Dove's Lesson

The nest began bulging
And soon I discovered
The two propped up high
Sitting out from under cover.

The Dove's Lesson

I knew as I watched
The day would soon come
When the dove family showcase
Would flee with the sun.

The Dove's Lesson

One day they sat perching
All three side by side.
In a moment's passing breeze
The Mother's wings began to flutter.

The Dove's Lesson

Taking a flight of five feet,
To the closest of branches,
Still, she sat waiting
As the young ones contemplated the chances.

The Dove's Lesson

Their flight was completed
And more short hops followed.
The trees filled with coos
While the tree fork looked hollow.

The Dove's Lesson

I looked at the empty nest
Resolved in the knowledge
That I had been blessed;
That gave me some solace.

For I missed the dear doves
And the delight of each day
Watching wings unfolding
And feathers changing colors.

The Dove's Lesson

But I had seen how the Mother nested,
Raised her babies, lived her life
And how she knew it was time
To lead the babies onward and upward.

The Dove's Lesson

And I watched how the baby doves
Took their early flight,
Abandoning all security
Knowing they were right.

The Dove's Lesson

The dove taught these lessons
I was privileged to see
When the Mother and babies
Outgrew their tree.

The Dove's Lesson

So when change brings discomfort
And security escapes you
Or the family moves onward
And the pain overtakes you,

The Dove's Lesson

Remember the dove's lesson.
From the nest it's safe for all to take wing.
You're ready for flight,
Well prepared for all coming things.

The Dove's Lesson

And listen for the dove.
The coos have a message.
To those who have been taught,
They say "Never fear; soar the heavens!"

The Dove's Lesson

Afterword

A mother dove made her nest and raised her babies in a tree outside our upstairs living room window. I set up a tripod and camera that remained there during the three to four weeks that the family occupied the nest. Each morning, my first activity was to check the nest. At noon and after work, I ran home eager to see the dove family. Although they were only four to five feet from me as I peered from the window, they seemingly took no notice. One weekend, I was away and I feared they'd be gone when I returned because the babies had been perching on the limbs outside the nest just before I left. When I arrived home, I raced to the nest. The little family began playing in the branches and within no more than thirty minutes, they took to flight, never to return to the nest again. I watched the empty nest for days with sad regret that they were gone. Feeling the loss, one day this poem came to me about what I'd been privileged to see.

The Dove's Lesson

The Dove's Lesson